目录

CONTENTS

目录

序

余福洲

天设地造的桂林山水以其秀丽与神奇，启迪了古往今来多少骚人墨客艺术创造的灵感？

我们不难想象，当华南第一岭那繁密的原始森林藏匿了大片的高山湿地，孕育了千万涓涓细流，造就了无数峡谷山涧，由此汇成的漓江一时吟唱，一时呼啸，经过无数卵石、细沙的净身，终于有了那无瑕的纯洁，滋养了两岸的长林丰草，雕凿了千姿百态的山峦青峰。当漓江敞开自己的胸怀，以心的静谧与世人对话之时，人们的所有的梦幻之门随之打开了。于是，那山水的云雾缭绕和烟雨迷蒙，给了人们飘逸的遐思、凝重的蕴意和生情的天趣；于是，那竹筏渔火和田园翠竹，描绘了人们毕生追求的悠悠远去又返回自心的境界，让人们实现追寻入世又融于自然的超越和创造外在形式与内在思绪统一的理想。

这就是桂林山水的自然性与人文意义的所在，这就是充满自然灵性与人文价值的桂林山水给予我们的摄影家和画家的艺术灵感的自然之源。

我们的摄影家就足履于桂林的山山水水，把新的审美发现记于一瞬间。这本集子有他们与山溪、硕石、峡谷的细语，有对阳光灿烂、明月淡照的叙说，也有对依山而建的吊脚楼的山寨和歌韵般感染力的梯田的抒发……这些摄影作品已经不是在简单地再现自然之美，而是在传递摄影家与山、水、云、雾、竹筏、红帆、田园、山寨的心灵碰撞而发出的悦耳的琴音，这正是我们希冀聆听的山水自然的天籁，正是我们渴求得到的山水自然具有永恒性的生命的活力。

而我们画家笔下的桂林山水，那又是画家将许多新的审美发现汇聚于心灵，慢慢地思索、咀嚼、消化，再经深挖、提炼，结果已不再是直面的山水物象，而是画家自己心灵的表现，是为大家构造的精神家园。

这本画册将摄影作品与绘画作品结集而出，可以让读者看到摄影家与画家的创造灵感是怎样同生于山水自然之源又怎样结果于不同的情感形式的。

PREFACE

Yu Fuzhou

How many literary figures and artists have been inspired by the charm and wonder of the paradise-like Guilin?

Just close your eyes and imagine. In the heart of the dense forests in the highest mountains of South China lays a large area of wetland where thousands of streams rise. Meandering through valleys and throwing themselves down cliffs, these streams converge into a mighty current-Lijiang River. Murmuring now and then, roaring here and where, the river roams through countless cobbles and grains of sand, unfolding its intact charm to the world. Alongside the river are exuberant trees, luxuriant vegetations, and grotesques hills. The river strikes out a quiet communication with the outside world, and dreams and fancies of millions of people are provoked. Exquisite hills and misty waters bestow upon poets and painters a mighty power of reason, of imagination, and an original sense of beauty; fishing rafts and green bamboo alongside the river picture a dreamland where man and nature enjoy a harmonious unity–an ideal that man has been dreaming about through ages.

Spontaneous and humane, Guilin landscape has become a life origin for many photographers and painters.

Traveling among hills and waters in Guilin, our photographers frame all the beautiful scenes with their cameras. This is an album from which we can hear their chat with the streams, rocks, and valleys. This is an album from which we can share their odes towards the sunshine and the moonlight. This is an album from which we can experience their passion for the mountain villages and the terraced fields...The pictures here are not simply a copy of the natural scenes, but insights of our photographers drawn on hills, waters, clouds, mists, bamboo-rafts, red sails, fields and mountain villages. The pictures here present us a full display of nature, with every detail original and every part true to life.

In the Chinese paintings, Guilin landscape has become the expressions of the artists' inner world. Having made a friend of nature, the painters perceive her in their mind's eye. Refined and distilled, these paintings are not merely images of landscape, but expressions of the painters' innermost, a dreamland that man has been longing for.

This album is a collection of pictures and paintings, from which we are able to learn how both the photographers and painters draw their inspirations from the same landscape, but express themselves in different ways.

序

余福洲

自然が創りあげた桂林山水の情景は、昔から今日まで、その秀麗さと神秘さでどれほど多くの詩人墨客の芸術創造意欲を掻き立ててきたことでしようか。

この華南第一のうっそうとした原始林は、広大な高山湿地を内に抱き、万を数える細流をはぐくみ、無数の渓谷を造りました。これらが集まってできあがった漓江は、時には歌い時には叫び声をあげながら、栗石や砂で浄化され、清らかな水となり両岸の草林を養い、千姿百態の青峰を彫り上げました。漓江が自らの懐を開き、心静かに人々に語りかけるとき、人間のあらゆる幻夢の扉は開かれるのです。あの山水を包み込む雲霧や朦朧とした煙雨の風景は、私たちに遥か遠くへの思いを抱かせ、心の奥の意識や自然の趣をもたらしてくれます。また、竹筏の漁火や田園の翠竹の風景は、生涯追い求めている悠揚さやいずれは自身の心に戻るという境地を描き出しています。そして人々が世俗の世界に入りつつも、超越した自然に融合する、つまり形と心を統一するという理想を実現させてくれます。

これが桂林山水には自然性と人的なものと存在しているということであり、自然性と人文価値にあふれた桂林山水が私たち写真家や画家に与えている芸術的霊感の源なのです。

私たち写真家は桂林山水を歩き回り、新しい美しさを発見すると瞬時に記録に留めます。この本には山渓、石、峡谷とのささやきがあり、太陽の輝きや名月の明かりに対する叙述があります。或いはまた山に寄り添って建った吊脚楼の山村や歌の調べのような棚田の叙情…があります。これらの写真は自然美の簡単な再現ではなくて、写真家が山、水、雲、霧、竹筏、赤い帆、田園、山村の心にめぐり遇って見つけ出した心地よい音色を伝えています、私たちが聞きたいと思っている山水自然の天籟であり、私たちが求めて止まない山水自然の持つ永遠の生命力を表現しています。

一方画家の筆による桂林水山も、多くの新たな美しさを発見し魂の中に集約させた上で、ゆっくりと思索、咀嚼、消化し、そして再び掘り起こし精錬したもので、それは目前にあるそのままの山水風景ではなく、画家自身の心を表現したものであり、誰もが持っている心の園であります。

この画集は写真作品と絵画作品とを組み合わせて出來上がったものですが、読者は写真家と画家の創造感覚が山水自然の原点の下でどのように生まれ、表現においてどのよう異なった情感形式となるかを見てとることができます。

桂林城区 THE CITY OF GUILIN 桂林市内

桂林是中国著名的风景旅游城市和历史文化名城，她拥有得天独厚的美丽的自然风光，有着悠久的历史文化，自秦始皇三十三年(前214)开凿灵渠，沟通湘、漓二水，桂林便成为南连海域、北达中原的重镇。西汉元鼎六年(前111)，汉武帝设始安县在今天的桂林。千百年来，桂林承袭了灿烂丰富的文化遗产，形成了集文、史、书、画等与自然风光和谐共存的独特的山水文化。许多吟咏桂林山水的不朽诗句，如"江作青罗带，山如碧玉簪"、"桂林山水甲天下"等已成为脍炙人口的千古绝唱。置身于美丽的桂林，可谓处处皆景：象山、叠彩山、独秀峰、伏波山、塔山等均是旅游观光的名山景点，泛舟于由两江四湖构成的环城水系，可尽览桂林城的风光名胜。

A well-known resort and a famous historical cultural city in China, Guilin enjoys a reputation for her unique landscape and long history. In the year of 214 B.C., Qing Shihuang, the first emperor of Qing Dynasty, ordered that the Ling Canal be dug to link Xiangjiang River and Lijiang River, thus making Guilin an important town bridging South China Sea and Central China. In the year of 111 B.C., Emperor Hanwu in West Han Dynasty instructed that Shi'an county be established. Thousands of years having passed, Guilin has become a city with a splendid cultural heritage, a city in which natural surroundings and human civilization stay in perfect unity. Cultural relics are to be found in every corner of the city, and fantastic poems in praise of Guilin have been read on from generation to generation, of which lines such as "rivers wind like ribbons of blue silk, and hills lie like hairpins of green jade", and "the landscape of Guilin is matchless in China" are the most famous. Hills dot here and there in the city, among which the Elephant Hill, the Piled Silk Hill, Solitary Beautiful Peak, Fubo Hill, and Pagoda Hill are well-known tourist attractions. A waterway connecting two rivers and four lakes zigzags through the city. Riding a boat on the waterway, tourists can enjoy the picturesque scenes in Guilin. Rightly is Guilin named as the city that is "surrounded by numerous hills and embraced by a waterway".

桂林は中国の有名な風景観光都市であり､また歴史文化の名城でもあります｡恵まれた美しい自然風光とあわせ悠久の歴史文化を持ち､秦の始皇帝33年(紀元前214年)から霊渠を開鑿し､湘漓の二水を結び南の海域や北の中原の都市と繋がることとなりました｡西漢元鼎6年(紀元前111年)、漢の武帝が今日の桂林に始安県を設けたのが桂林の始まりです｡その後長きにわたり桂林は輝く文化遺産を継承しながら､文､史､書､画等と自然風光とが調和共存した独自の山水文化を形成してきました。桂林山水を吟した不朽の詩句は数多くあります｡例えば「江作青羅帯､山如碧玉簪」(川は青き絹の帯を作り、山は緑の玉の簪の如し)、或いは「桂林山水甲天下」(桂林の山水は天下に甲たり)などの表現は多くの人に知られているところです｡この美しい桂林に立ってみると、至る所すべてが風光の地であると言っても過言ではありません｡すなわち象山､畳彩山､独秀峰､伏波山､塔山等それぞれが観光の名勝地であります｡両江四湖の環状水系をなしています｡乗船し川の上から桂林の名勝風光を味わうことができます。

桂林城区风光
Guilin downtown scenery
桂林城区の風光

象鼻山 位于漓江与桃花江汇流处，山形酷似一头巨象伸长鼻临江汲水。江水穿洞而过，山洞如明月浮水，构成天下独一无二的“象山水月”景观。宋代蓟北处士《水月洞》诗赞道：“水底有明月，水上明月浮，水流月不去，月去水还流。”象山以其栩栩如生的形象，被视为桂林山水的代表，桂林城的象征。

ELEPHANT HILL Located at the joining point of Lijiang River and Peach Blossom River, Elephant Hill looks exactly like a giant elephant gulping the crystal-clear water. Water runs through the big round tunnel between its trunk and body, which resembles a full moon floating on the river. This unique scene is called “Water Moon of Elephant Hill”. A poet in Song Dynasty vividly described this scene in his poem *Moon Floating on Water*. The lines are as follows: “A full moon is seen deep in water; A full moon is seen floating on river; The river keeps running but the moon stays; The moon is gone but the water is still on move.” Now the Elephant Hill has become a popular scenic spot for tourists and the symbol of Guilin city itself.

象鼻山 漓江と桃花江との合流點にあり、その山の形は一頭の巨象が鼻を伸ばし川から水を飲んでいる姿によく似ています。川の水が洞窟を穿ち、その形は明月のように水に浮かび、この世に二つとない「象山水月」の景観を作り出しています。宋代の薊北処士は「水月洞」と題した詩の中で次のように讃えています。「水底に明月あり、水上に明月浮かぶ、水流るも月去らず、月去るも水なお流る」と。象山はその生き生きとした形から、桂林山水の代表、象徴として認められています。

象山晨雾
Morning Fog Around Elephant Hill
象山の朝霧

象山雪
Snow Scene of Elephant Hill
象山の雪景

象山之夜
Night Scene of Elephant Hill
象山の夜

象鼻山
Elephant Hill
象鼻山

花桥
Flower Bridge
花橋

榕湖玻璃桥
Glass Bridge on Ronghu Lake
榕湖の玻璃橋

漓江大瀑布酒店
Lijiang Grand Waterfall Hotel
漓江大瀑布飯店

骆驼山秋色
Autumn Scene of Camel Hill
駱駝山の秋模様

叠彩风光　Piled Silk Hill 畳彩山の風光

叠彩山　古称桂山，由四望山、于越峰、明月峰与仙鹤峰四峰组成，山上岩层呈厚层、中厚层及薄层状，远望似彩绸相叠，故以为名。沿石梯登上主峰明月峰山顶拿云亭，可一览桂林市区概貌。山上有一风洞，有210件古今石刻集中分布在洞内外。

PILED SILK HILL　Once called Cassia Hill, this hill is made up by four peaks (Siwang Peak, Yuyue Peak, Crane Peak and Bright Moon Peak). The hill has places broken, and strata are exposed here and there, revealing a distinct classification of three layers, with the bottom being the thickest and the top one the thinnest. Looked from a distance, the strata are just like piled-up silks and satins, thus the hill got its present name. Climbing up along the stone steps to the top of the main peak, the Bright Moon Peak, tourists can have a bird's-eye view of the city from the "Catch-Cloud Pavilion". A wind tunnel, in and out of which 210 pieces of ancient and modern stone carvings distribute, is to be found near the hilltop.

畳彩山　古くは桂山と呼ばれ、四望山、于越峰、明月峰及び仙鶴峰の四峰からなっています。山上の岩層は厚層、中厚層、薄層状のものがあり、遠くから見ると色絹を重ね合わせた形に似ているのでこの名前が付けられました。石段に沿って主峰の明峰山頂の拿雲亭に登ると、桂林市街の様子が一望できます。山上には一つの洞があり、210件の古今の石刻がその洞の内外に集中的に分布しています。

伏波山 位于滨江路北端的漓江西岸，孤峰突起，西枕陆地，东临漓江，有遏波伏澜之势，因唐代曾在山上修建了以汉朝伏波将军马援命名的马援祠而得名。伏波山公园集山、水、洞、石、亭、园、文物等于不足1万平方米的范围内，成为独特的桂林山水的缩影。

FUBO HILL Located at the north end of Binjiang Avenue, the hill towers on the west side of Lijiang River. With its base half in water in the east and half on land in the west, the hill seems to attempt to tame the surging waves in the river. There used to be a temple on the hill. The temple was built in Tang Dynasty in memory of the Fubo general, MaYuan, after whom the hill was named. With an area of no more than 10,000 square meters, Fubo Hill Park amasses a lot of attractions, including a graceful hill, pretty pavilions, rolling waves, fantastic caves, grotesque stones, neat gardens, and cultural relics, known as the epitome of Guilin landscape.

伏波山 浜江路北端の漓江両岸にあります。孤峰が突起しており、西は陸地に臨み、東は漓江に面しています。大波を鎮める地勢があり、唐代に山上に漢朝伏波将軍馬援が命名した馬援祠が建てられたことによりこの名前がついています。伏波山公園は、約1万m^2足らずの範囲内に、山、水、洞、石、亭、文物を集めた特色ある桂林山水の縮景となっています。

伏波山
Fubo Hill
伏波山

独秀峰 又称紫金山。位于市区王城内，山峰平地拔起，雄伟俊秀，有“南天一柱”之誉。从西麓登山，共306级，拾级而上形成了三个转折，每一个山弯景观各有不同，到达山顶，登上独秀亭，纵目四望，峰林环立，绿水萦回，全城秀色，尽浮眼底。

SOLITARY BEAUTY PEAK Once called Zijin Hill, this hill towers in the Prince's Palace in the downtown area. Rising abruptly on the ground, Solitary Beauty Peak enjoys a fame of being "the Number One Pillar in South China". Climbing up along the 306 stone steps from the west bottom of the hill, tourists are to meet three turnings, at each of which a different scene comes into view. A pavilion (Solitary Beauty Pavilion) on the hilltop offers a good place for sightseeing, from which tourists can see a full picture of Guilin city, with green peaks dotting here and there, and clear waters winding their ways through the downtown area.

独秀峰 別名「紫金山」と呼ばれ、市内の古王城内にあります。平地から突き出した峰は勇壮な形をし「南天の一柱」の誉があります。西の麓から登ると合わせて306段の階段があり，石段を一段一段上っていくと、3度の曲がり角があり、どの位置からの景観も異なっています。山頂の独秀亭に立ち四方を眺めると、峰峰が環状に聳え立ち、緑水がめぐらされ、町全体が美しくいつまでも目に浮かんできます。

独秀峰 Solitary Beauty Peak 独秀峰

塔山 Pagoda Hill 塔山

新桂林秀色
A Glimpse of New Guilin
新桂林の美しい模様

两江四湖 即漓江、桃花江、木龙湖、桂湖、榕湖、杉湖。由两江四湖构成的环城水系，襟江接湖，山环水绕，乘舟环江湖蜿蜒而行，名胜风光尽览其中。每当夕阳西下，万盏齐明，湖岸彩灯点点，桥跨银河，双塔映月，如诗如梦，令游人心醉神迷，流连忘返。

TWO RIVER AND FOUR LAKES

This is a round-the-city waterway linking the two rivers (Lijiang River and Peach Blossom River) and the four lakes (Ronghu Lake, Shanhu Lake, Mulong Lake and Guihu Lake). Riding a boat, tourists can enjoy all sorts of interesting things. When night falls and lights on, the waterway unfolds the other facet of the city. With color lights twinkling along the banks, bridges illuminated in neon light, and the Twin Pagodas bathing in the moonlight, the waterway becomes so fantastic that tourists are likely to forget where they are and become lost.

両江四湖 漓江、桃花江、木龍湖、桂湖、榕湖、杉湖の二つの川と四つの湖が街を取り巻く水系を構成することにより、川と湖がつながり、山の周囲を水がめぐることとなり、船に乗って江湖を回ることができるようになりました。名勝風光がその中に尽くされています。夕日が西に沈む頃になると万灯のあかり、湖岸の彩灯が点火され、銀河にかかる橋、双塔映月などまさに幻想の世界となり、旅人たちを酔わせ名残おしさを感じさせています。

杉湖双塔 又称日月双塔，分别为铜塔及琉璃塔，位于杉湖东南侧，铜塔共九层，高41米，自湖中升腾而起。琉璃塔建于杉湖岛上，共七层，高35米。两塔通过水下的水族馆相连通。现在，该双塔已成为市中心的旅游新景观及游人观赏城市美景最佳胜地之一。

TWIN PAGODAS OF SHANHU LAKE One bronze and the other glazed, the Twin Pagodas are also called the Sun Pagoda and the Moon Pagoda. Tall and erect on the southeast of Shanhu Lake, the two pagodas are connected with each other through an aquarium under water. The 9-storey bronze pagoda is built in water, with a height of 41 meters. The 7-storey glazed pagoda is 35 meters high, and it is built on Shanhu Island. Now one of the most popular tourist attractions in the downtown area, the Twin Pagodas prove to be really eye-catching.

杉湖双塔 日月双塔とも呼んでいます。銅塔と瑠璃塔の2つに分かれ、杉湖の東南側に位置している。銅塔は9層からなり41mの高さがあり湖中から聳え立ち二つの世界一を持っています。すなわち世界で最も高い銅塔、最高の銅製建築物及び最高の水中塔であることです。瑠璃塔は杉湖島上に立ち7層からなり高さは35mです。二つの塔は水面下の水族館を通して相通じています。現在この二つの塔は市中心部の新しい観光名所となっています。

金银双塔夜景
Night Scene of the Twin Pagodas
金銀双塔の夜の景色

桂林梦幻之夜
Dream-Like Night of Guilin
桂林夢幻の夜

古南门 又名榕树门，建于南宋。古南门前有一株树龄八百余年的大榕树，浓荫覆盖，一年四季郁郁苍苍，与古南门构成“榕城古荫”一景。

OLD CITY GATE This gate was built in South Song Dynasty. With a big banyan tree over eight hundred years old growing in front, the gate has also acquired the name of Banyan Gate. With exuberant foliage and thick shades all the year around, the old banyan tree gives a new look to the ancient city gate, and this scene is thus called “Old Banyan at the City Gate”.

古南門 別名「榕樹門」といい、南宋の頃に建てられました。古南門の前には樹齢800余年の大榕樹があります。濃い緑色で年中覆われ、古南門とともに「榕樹古蔭」の一景となっています。

古南门之夜
Night Scene of Old City Gate
古南門の夜

桂湖丽泽桥夜景
Night Scene of Lize Bridge on Guihu Lake
桂湖麗沢橋の夜景

三桥夜景
Night Scene of the Three Bridges
三橋の夜景

宋城之夜
Night Scene of Song City
宋城の夜景

尧山云海
Clouds over Yao Mountain
堯山の雲海

尧山　位于桂林市东北，距市中心约 10 公里，主峰海拔 909.3 米，是桂林市区最高的山峰，因周唐时在西坡建有尧帝庙而得名。尧山山体高大雄浑，山峦起伏，气势磅礴，植物丰茂，杜鹃遍野。尧山山麓，有明代的靖江王墓群，是国内保存完好的明代藩王墓群，规模宏大。

YAO MOUNTAIN Located in the east suburb and about ten kilometers away from the city center, the mountain ranks the first in height in the urban areas, whose highest peak reaches to 909.3 meters above sea level. The mountain got its name from the temple that was built on the west mountainside in Zhou-Tang Period to commemorate Yao Emperor. Grandeur and magnificent, Yao Mountain stretches miles away, covered by thick forests and azaleas. At the foot of the Yao Mountain, tourists cannot miss out on the grand Jingjiang Mausoleum, where the prince in Ming Dynasty was buried. Jingjiang Mausoleum is known to be one of the best-protected Ming tombs in China.

堯山　桂林市の北東10キロのところにあり、主峰の海抜は903.3mです。堯山は桂林市で最も高い山で、唐代に西側山腹に堯帝廟が建てられたことによりこの名前がつけられました。堯山の全容は、高く雄大で起伏に富み、広大無辺の勢いがあります。また植物は繁茂し、ホトトギスが野を巡り、山麓にある明代の靖江王墓群は、国内でも規模が大きく保存良好な王墓群です。

桂海碑林 位于七星公园月牙山瑶光峰南麓，由龙隐洞、龙隐岩两处石刻组成，此处“壁无突石”，碑刻如林，碑林共有从唐至魏的楷、草、隶、篆等书体石刻220余件。其中最为著名的是宋刻《元祐党籍碑》，龙隐岩口还建有桂海碑林陈列馆，展示分布于全市的碑刻拓片，被誉为“古代书法艺林”。

FOREST OF STELES Located at the south foot of Yaoguang Peak of Crescent Hill in Seven-Star Park, this scenic spot is made up by inscriptions and carvings both in the Dragon Hidden Cave and on the Dragon Hidden Rocks. Inscriptions and carvings scatter everywhere on the surface of smooth rocks, the total number of which amounts to more than 220 pieces, including calligraphy inscriptions of various styles finished in a time period from Tang Dynasty to Wei Dynasty. The most famous stele here is the “Yuanyou Party Record” finished in Song Dynasty. At the entrance of the Dragon Hidden Cave is an exhibition hall, where steles collected form other places of Guilin are on display.

桂海碑林 七星公園の月牙山瑶光峰の南麓にあります。龍隠洞、龍隠岩の石刻からなりたっています。ここの壁は平らで碑刻が林のように並んでいます。碑林は唐から魏にかけてのもので、楷書、草書、隷書、篆書など220余件あります。そのうち最も有名なものは、宋代の石刻〈元祐党籍碑〉です。龍隠岩の入り口には桂海碑林陳列館があり、全市の碑刻拓本を展示しており、「古代書道芸林」として賞賛されています。

桂海碑林
Forest of Steles
桂海碑林

摩崖石刻雕像
Rock Carvings
摩崖石の彫刻像

伏波山试剑石
Sword Testing Stone of Fubo Hill
伏波山の試剣石

漓江 LIJIANG RIVER 漓江

漓江发源于海拔2141.5米的猫儿山，自桂林至阳朔83公里水程，被誉为百里画廊。清澈的江水如一条透迤流转的碧绿绸带，环绕于万千奇峰之间，形态各异的青峰夹岸耸立，尽展妩媚的仙姿神态……冠岩、半边渡、杨堤、下龙、九马画山、黄布滩、兴坪、渔村等，是漓江山水画长卷中精彩纷呈的片段和高潮。

Rising from the 2141.5 meter high Mao'er Mountain, Xing'an County, the 83-kilometer-long Lijiang River from Guilin to Yangshuo is reputed as a picture gallery. Like a jade ribbon, the crystal-clear river winds its way forward with hills of various shapes lining up on the banks. Scenic spots such as Crown Cave, One-Side Ferry, Yangdi Village, Xialong Bend, Nine-Horse Fresco Hill, Yellow Cloth Beach, Xingping Town, and Fishing Village are to be found in this part of the waterway, which is known to be the best of the gallery.

漓江は海抜2141.5mの猫児山に源を発し、桂林から陽朔までの間83kmは「百里の画廊」と賞されています。清冽な水の流れは、うねり曲がる緑絹の帯のように万を数える奇峰の間を巡り、様々な形をした青峰は川の両岸に聳え柔らかな神仙の姿を現わしています。川岸の緑竹が風に揺れ、川面には山峰が倒影し漁舟が点々としています…冠岩、綉山、半辺渡、楊堤、下龍湾、九馬画山、黄布灘、興坪、漁村等は漓江山水絵巻の中で出色的な場面絶頂です。

静静的漓江
Tranquil Lijiang River
漓江の静寂

山高水远
High Mountains and a Distant River
山高水遠

漓江红帆
Red Sails on Lijiang River
漓江紅い帆

奇峰镇 位于桂林市区南郊10公里处的东山村，这里奇峰林立，山势峭拔，山下阡陌田畴纵横交错，村落散布其间。春耕时节，水田如镜，倒映群峰；秋天金风送爽，激起千层稻浪，如诗如画。

QIFENG TOWN Located about 10 kilometers away in the south suburb of Guilin is a village called Dongshan. With hills of fantastic shapes dotting around and fields crisscrossed by footpaths, this place proves to be very eye-catching. In spring, the mirror-like paddy fields reflect the surrounding peaks; Autumn finds the crops waving in gentle breeze, thus the village becomeing a fairyland.

奇峰鎮 桂林市の南郊10kmのところの東山村にあります。奇峰が林立し、天高く抜き出ており、幾重もの層を成しています。麓の畦道や田畑は縦横に交錯し、民家がその間に散らばっています。春耕の時には水田は鏡のように如く群峰を投影し、秋の風が吹くと幾層もの稲穂が波打ちます、山里は詩画のようです。

暮归
Back Home in Twilight
暮帰

晨光
Morning Sun
朝の光

冠岩江口　冠岩位于草坪乡的冠山下，它是一个巨型地下河洞穴，该溶洞交错重叠，曲折幽深。洞内悬布着绚丽异常的石钟乳、石笋、石幔、石柱、石花等。临江有一洞口，一股清流从那里流出，汇入漓江。从洞口观赏漓江景色，别有洞天之趣。

CROWN CAVE　Winding its way through Crown Hill in Caoping is the Crown Cave, one of the longest and largest caves in Asia. Inside the cave is a subterranean stream murmuring along, and stalactites, stalagmites, stone curtains, stone pillars, and stone flowers are seen everywhere. The stream meanders through stones to join Lijiang River at the entrance of the cave. Watching Lijiang River from here, tourists can have quite a different view.

冠岩江口　冠岩は草坪郷の冠山の下にある巨大な地下川の鍾乳洞です。この鍾乳洞は幾十にも交錯し、曲がりくねっています。洞内には絢爛多彩な鍾乳石、石筍、石帷、石柱、石花があります。漓江に臨む洞口から清流が流れ出ており人々を引き付けています。洞口から見る漓江の景色は、また一種違った趣があります。

冠岩江口
Entrance of Crown Cave
冠岩の江口

下龙筏影
Scene of Xialong Bend, Lijiang River
下龍の筏影

下龙 漓江流经这里拐了一道90度的弯，江岸竹林繁茂，奇峰耸立，倒影如画，渔舟穿行于江心，白鹭在青山绿水间盘旋。不知不觉间，夕阳西下，余晖将山峰映得金黄，在蓝天下熠熠发光，山脚下的村落，炊烟已袅袅升起。

XIALONG BEND Lijiang River takes a sharp turn here and forms a bend. The river in this part unfolds a fascinating scene before the tourists' eyes–tall and dense bamboo line up alongside the river, and reflections of the hills in the water are extremely charming. The fishing boats are drift on the river, and egrets are flying among the peaks. The sun is about to set, coloring the hilltops with a touch of gold, and smoke is seen to curl upward from the kitchen chimneys in the village.

下龍 漓江の流れはここから90度に曲がります。両岸では竹の林が繁茂し、奇峰は聳え立ち水影は絵画のようです。漁舟は川の中心を進んでいます。白鷺は青山緑水の間を旋回し、いつの間にか夕日が西に沈む頃、夕焼けが山峰を黄金色に映し出し、青空の下で光輝いています。山麓の村ではかまどの煙がたなびき始めます。

竹映漓江
Bamboo Alongside Lijiang River
竹映の漓江

江畔阳光
Bathing in the Sun

杨堤 位于距桂林城区约46公里的漓江西岸，杨堤村后有一座山名为羊蹄山，山的两个峰像一对倒挂的羊蹄，当地人取之谐音作为村名。杨堤两岸翠竹婆娑，座座青峰掩映其后，与青山、绿水、飞瀑、浅滩相映成趣。

YANGDI VILLAGE Situated forty-six kilometers away from downtown Guilin on the west bank of Lijiang River is Yangdi Village. Located behind the village is a hill that looks like a pair of goat hooves hanging upside down. "Goat hooves" and "Yangdi" are pronounced the same in Chinese language, and thus the locals named the hill and their village. Here green bamboo dance in breeze alongside the river, and pretty peaks keep their mysterious looks half hidden behind the bamboo. Green hills, clear water, flying waterfalls and shallow beaches turn the place into a well-known tourist attraction.

楊堤 桂林から約46km離れた漓江の西岸にあります。楊堤村の背後には羊蹄山と名つけられた山があり、その二つの峰がちょうど逆さになった羊の蹄に似ていることから、村人は同じ発音である楊堤という村名をつけました。楊堤両岸の緑竹がゆらゆらと揺れ、後方の青峰を時にさえぎり、青山、緑水、飛瀑、浅瀬と相映り趣をなしています。

漓江墨韵
A Typical Chinese Painting
漓江の墨韵

漓江晨渡
Morning Ferry
漓江の朝の渡す

晨色
Morning Scene
朝の色

千峰映飞虹　Rainbow on the Mountain Tops　群峰に映る虹

黄布滩筏影
Bamboo Raft at Yellow Cloth Beach
黄布灘の筏影

黄布滩　因江底有黄石如布而得名，这里江流清澈宁静，云山倒影，如诗似梦，两岸耸立着七座大小不一的山峰，宛如七位浴水而出的少女，人称“七仙下凡”。黄布滩是观看青峰倒影的最佳处。

YELLOW CLOTH BEACH　A large yellowish rock stretches itself in this part of the river. Viewed from above, the rock looks like a piece of yellow cloth swaying in the water flow. Alongside the river stand seven pretty peaks, commonly known as *Seven Fairies Descending to the Human World* in a Chinese legend. Water here is as smooth as mirror, making it the best place for tourists to watch reflections.

黄布灘　川底の黄色い石板が布に似ているところからこの名がつけられました。この辺りの流れは澄みきったうえ静かであるため雲や山の水影は詩画のようです。両岸に聳える大小７つの山峰は、水を浴びて出てきた７人の少女のようであり、人々から「七仙下凡」(七仙人が俗世間に下る)と呼ばれています。黄布灘は青峰の水影を見るのに絶好の場所です。

漓江冬景　Winter Scene of Lijiang River　漓江の冬景色

九马画山
Nine-Horse Fresco Hill
九馬画山

九马画山 过二郎峡、大�滩，河水右弯，江东岸五峰相连的青山就是九马画山。山西面削壁临江，高宽百余米的巨大石壁直插江底，崖壁上青绿黄白的图纹依稀可辨出九匹姿态各异的骏马，或立或卧，或奔或跃，或饮或嘶，形神毕肖。

NINE-HORSE FRESCO HILL Flowing past the Erlang Gorge and Dasang Beach, the river turns right, and a mountain range with five peaks connecting with each other come into the tourists' view. This is known to be the Nine-Horse Fresco Hill. Located on the east bank, the mountain unfolds its large cliff face abruptly to the river. Over 100 meters in height and width, the cliff bears shades of various colors which resemble nine horses in different postures. They are either standing, lying, running, prancing, neighing or gulping.

九馬画山 二郎峡、大磉灘を過ぎて川の水が右に曲がるところ、川の東岸に5峰が連なる青山が九馬画山です。川に面した山の西面壁は、100m余りある巨大な垂直の岩壁で、その表面は青、緑、黄、白色の色模様が鮮やかで、9匹の姿の異なる駿馬を描き出しています。立っている馬、横になっている馬、走っている馬、跳ねている馬、水を飲んでいる馬、いなないている馬など形よく似ています。

清澈的漓江
Crystal-Clear Lijiang River
清い漓江

朝笏山
Tablet Hill
朝笏山

烟雨漓江
Lijiang River in Misty Rain
漓江の煙雨

竹筏待出
Ready-to-go Bamboo Raft
待出の竹筏

点火 Lighting a Fire 火をつける

漓江鸬鹚 俗称鱼鹰，漓江两岸的渔民，大都用鸬鹚捕鱼。他们撑着竹排，带着鸬鹚，穿行于江面，鸬鹚发现鱼情会迅猛地跳下江中，潜入水底，捕捉鱼儿后再跳上竹排。

CORMORANTS ON LIJIANG RIVER Most of the fishermen living alongside Lijiang River keep cormorants to assist them in fishing. With cormorants sitting on the bamboo rafts, the fishermen begin their busy day. Once the cormorants find fish, they dive swiftly into the water, and in a second they jump out onto the rafts, fish in mouth.

漓江の鵜飼 漓江両岸の漁民は、たいてい鵜を使って魚を捕ります。竹竿を手に鵜を連れて川面に漕ぎ出します。鵜は魚の気配を察すると勢く水中に飛び込み、水底に潜り込みます。一瞬のうちに嘴に銀色に光る魚をくわえて竹ざおに飛び上がるのです。

撒网
Casting a Net
網を打つ

兴坪 距今已有1300年的历史，是漓江百里画廊的风光荟萃之地，登老寨山可观小河背日出，一览小镇全景；伫立码头远眺骆驼过江，看晚霞落日；上游不远处有僧尼山、朝笏山，下游有螺蛳山，在古镇东北方有莲花岩。

XINGPING TOWN With a history of 1300 years. Clustering around this part of Lijiang River are magnificent scenes. Tourists can either mount Laozai Hill to watch the sun rise from Back of Litter River and get a bird's eye view of Xingping Town, or stand at the ferry to enjoy the beautiful sunset and a scene called "Camels Wading Across the River". Not far ahead up the river are scenic spots such as the Nun Hill and the Tablet Hill, and down the river is the Conch Hill. The Lotus Cave is located to the northwest of this ancient town.

興坪 興坪は1300年の歴史を持っています。漓江の興坪は風景が集約された土地で、老寨山に登ると川の向こうに日の出を見ることができ、村全体が一望できます。また船着場に立って遠く駱駝過川を眺めると霞にけむる夕日が見えます。ここから上流遠くないところには僧尼山、朝笏山、下流に行けば螺螄山があります。古村の東北には蓮花岩もあります。

兴坪之晨
Morning Scene of Xingping
興坪の朝

兴坪胜境　Picturesque Xingping　興坪の景勝

漓江写生
Sketching by Lijiang River
漓江写生

漓江的美丽景色，吸引了无数的摄影家、画家，他们的镜头和画笔为这条美丽的漓江留下了无数令人赏心悦目的艺术佳作。

The unique landscape alongside Lijiang River appeals to many photographers and artists, who, with their cameras and brushes, have framed and recorded many a beautiful scene.

漓江の美しい景色は多くの写真家、画家を惹きつけました。彼らのレンズや絵筆は、その美しい漓江を表現する、人の心や目を楽しませる芸術作品を残しました。

晨光照漓江 Lijiang River in the Morning Sun 漓江の朝日

从兴坪的漓江东岸观赏漓江风光，但见奇峰耸立，翠竹摇风，江流婉转，渔舟点点，山清水秀的天然画景呈现在眼前，这里就是20元人民币风景图案中的画面实景。

Looking from the eastern bank of Lijiang River by Xingping Town, tourists can have a spectacular view–grotesque hills dotting here and there, green bamboo nodding in the breeze, and fishing boats drifting on the gentle water. This is the place whose delicate view has been printed onto the note of 20 *yuan* RMB.

興坪の漓江東岸から漓江の風景を眺めると、奇峰が聳え立ち、翠竹が風にそよぎ、川の流れは蛇行し、漁舟が点在するという山紫水明の天然画が眼前に迫ります。この地は20元札に描かれた図案の元の風景です。

渔村 位于鲤鱼山对岸的漓江东侧，渔村的大部分民居建于明正德年间(1506~1521)，来到渔村，随渔民出船打鱼，过一回渔民生活，品尝肉质鲜嫩的漓江鱼，自是别有一番情趣。1998年，美国总统克林顿先生访华专程到渔村民家做客。孙中山先生当年挥师北伐途经桂林时，也曾在此驻足。

THE FISHING VILLAGE Built during the Zhengde Period(1506~1521) in Ming Dynasty, the village remains on the east bank of Lijiang River, opposite the Carp Hill on the other riverside. Tourists can have a short stay here to escape the bustle and hustle of life, and it is great fun to ride bamboo rafts and go fishing with the villagers. Bill Clinton, the U.S. president, paid the village a visit in 1998, and Mr. Sun Yat-sen also made a temporary stay here when he led the Northern Expeditionary Army to suppress Yuan Shikai.

漁村 鯉魚山の対岸、漓江の東岸に位置する漁村のほとんどの民家は明の正徳年間(1506～1521)に建てられたものです。漁村を訪れると、漁民とともに船に乗って魚を捕り、漁民生活を経験し、新鮮で柔らかい漓江魚を味わうことができます。これもまた一種の情緒であります。1998年アメリカのクリントン大統領が訪中の際、漁村の民家を訪問しました。また孫中山先生もかつて北伐途中で桂林を通過した時、ここで駐屯したことがあります。

螺蛳山远眺
A Distant View of Conch Hill
螺蛳山の遠望

渔村民居一角
A Glimpse of the Houses in the Fishing Village
漁村民家の風景

漓江渔女
Fishing Girls
漓江漁村の娘

漓江夜曲
Evening Scene of Lijiang River
漓江のセレナーデ

漓江渔火
Lights on Rafts
灕江漁火

漓江清夏
Summer Scene of Lijiang River
漓江の清夏

漓江奇峰
Grotesque Peaks Alongside Lijiang River
漓江の奇峰

工艺摊
Handicraft Shop
工芸店舗

西街之夜
Night Scene of West Street
西街の夜

阳朔西街 西街又称洋人街，位于阳朔县城中心的漓江西岸，约1千米青石板铺就的街道和古朴的岭南风格民居构成的西街，林立着酒吧、餐馆、旅店、工艺品店、网吧，等等。每天徜徉着无数中外游人，使阳朔古城变得别具风情。

WEST STREET It is also called the Foreigners' Street. Situated on the west bank of Lijiang River, the 1000-meter-long street stretches itself from east to west through the center of Yangshuo town. Covered with long slabs, and with houses of ancient styles lining up on each side, the street has become a popular place for many foreigners, where they can while away their time in bars, cafes, inns and handicraft shops.

陽朔西街 西街は洋人街とも呼ばれており、陽朔県の中心漓江の西岸にあります。約1kmにわたる長青石板の敷きつめられた通りと古風な嶺南風格をもった民家から構成されています。酒場、レストラン、旅館、工芸品店などが立ち並んでいます。毎日、多くの国内外からの観光客が往来しており、陽朔はまた違った風情をもっています。

西街阳光
West Street in the Sun
西街の陽光

江畔牧童
A Cowboy
江畔の牧童

印象·刘三姐 以阳朔书童山附近2公里的漓江水域和山峰为舞台和背景，以经典影片《刘三姐》为母题和素材，由张艺谋总导演打造的一场盛大的山水实景演出。在美丽的漓江边，在万籁俱静的晚上，美丽的山歌，美丽的山水和美丽的刘三姐，在纯自然的水光山色、月明星辉与现代化的灯光复合效果中，构成了一次次梦幻与真实的充满诗情画意的美妙旅程。

IMPRESSION · SINGER LIU SANJIE Landscape two kilometers around the Page Boy Hill as its stage, and story from the classical film *Singer Liu Sanjie* as its theme, the grand musical *Impression · Singer Liu Sanjie* directed by Zhang Yimou has been put on by Lijiang River. Surrounded by charming folk songs by beautiful girls at a quiet night, the audience is thrilled to find that they are enjoying a feast for both their eyes and ears.

印象・劉三姐 陽朔の書童山付近2kmの漓江水域と山峰を舞台背景に、また古典的映画『劉三姐』を原題、素材として、張芸謀総監督が大規模な山水実景の演出を行ないました。美しい漓江のほとりで、すべてが静まった夜に、美しい山歌と、山水風景、劉三姐が自然の水光山色、月明星輝と現代的な光とが混ぜ合わせた効果の中で、幻のような真実のような詩情画意あふれる美しい旅をかもし出します。

《印象 · 刘三姐》之夜
Impression · Singer Liu Sanjie
『印象 · 劉三姐』の夜

《印象 · 刘三姐》之夜
Impression · Singer Liu Sanjie
『印象 · 劉三姐』の夜

乡间小景
Country Scene
郷間の小景

富里桥
Fuli Bridge
富里橋

高田风光
Gaotian Scenery
高田の風光

木山民居　Mushan Residential Area　木山民家

小河背风光
Back of Little River
小河背の風光

大地之春
Spring Scene
大地の春

遇龙河风光 Meeting-Dragon River 遇龍河の風光

遇龙河 全长43.5公里，风光秀丽，被誉为小漓江。沿岸散落的村寨、古桥、古树与两岸的青山绿水、田园风光构成一幅充满了诗情画意的画卷，令游人领略到远离尘嚣，回归自然的美妙境界。

MEETING-DRAGON RIVER With a length of 43.5 kilometers, the river is considered to be an epitome of Lijiang River. Alongside the river are green hills and clear waters, with villages, ancient bridges and old trees dotting here and there, making it the best place to escape the bustle and hustle of the world.

遇龍河 全長は43.5km、風光明媚で小漓江と呼ばれています。岸にそって点在する村落や古橋、古樹が両岸の青山緑水、田園風景とあいまって詩情画意溢れる一幅の絵巻を作り上げ、訪れるものに世俗を忘れさせ素晴しい自然の境地を感じさせます。

大地春耕
Spring Plowing
大地の春の耕し

红色乐章
Lijiang River in Rosy Glow
赤い楽章

周边各县风光

SCENIC ATTRACTIONS IN THE NEARBY COUNTIES

周辺各県の風光

以桂林市区为中心半径约100公里的区域内，大小景点星罗棋布。主要的自然及人文景观有：灵川县的青狮潭，古东瀑布，大圩古镇及海洋的银杏林，龙胜县的梯田、温泉和花坪自然保护区，兴安县的灵渠、猫儿山，全州县的湘山寺、天湖，灌阳县的黑岩，平乐县的古榕林、车田石林，恭城县的文庙、武庙，荔浦县的银子岩、丰鱼岩，永福县的板峡水库，资源县的资江、宝鼎瀑布、八角寨，等等。随着旅游业的不断升温，资源境内特有的自然景观正吸引着越来越多的八方游客，逐渐成为新的旅游热点。

In the area within a 100-meter radius of downtown Guilin scatter a great variety of scenic spots. Places of natural and cultural interest include Qingshitan Reservoir in Lingchuan County, Gudong Waterfalls, Daxu Town, Ginkgo forest in Haiyang Township, Longsheng Terraced Fields, Longsheng Hot Springs, Huaping Nature Preserve, Ling Canal and Mao'er Mountain in Xing'an County, Xiangshan Temple and Heaven Lake in Quanzhou County, Dark Cave in Guanyang County, Zijiang River, Baoding Waterfall, and Bajiao Hamlet in Ziyuan County, Old Banyans Trees in Pingle County, Confucian Temple and Guan Yu Temple in Gongcheng County, Silver Cave and Fengyu Cave in Lipu County, and Banxia Reservoir in Yongfu County, etc. Now the spectacular landscape in Ziyuan County is attracting more and more tourists, and it has become one of the hot resorts.

桂林市を中心とする半径100km以内の区域には大小様々な観光拠点が星のごとく散らばっています。主な自然景観、人文景観としては、霊川県の青獅潭、古東瀑布、大圩古鎮、銀杏林、龍勝県の棚田、温泉、花坪自然保護区、興安県の霊渠、猫児山、全州県の湘山寺、天湖、灌陽県の黒岩、平楽県の古榕樹、車田石林、恭城県の文廟、武廟、荔浦県の銀子岩、豊魚岩、永福県の板峡ダム、資源県の資江、宝鼎瀑布、八角村等々があります。観光業のたゆまぬ発展向上に伴い、資源県内に特有の自然景観が現在多くの旅行客を惹きつけ新しい観光スポットになりつつあります。

猫儿山
Mao'er Mountain
猫児山

华江秋色
Autumn Scene of Huajiang
華江の秋模様

兴安灵渠
Ling Canal in Xing'an County
興安の霊渠

资江天门一景
A Glimpse of Zijiang River
資江天門の風景

宝鼎瀑布
Baoding Waterfall
宝鼎の滝

八角寨云海奇观
Clouds Above Bajiao Hamlet
八角寨の雲海奇峰

龙胜梯田 梯田景区位于龙胜县和平乡境内，分为龙脊梯田和金坑梯田两大景区。梯田如练似带，从山脚盘绕至山顶，彼此连绵起伏，一气呵成。“春飘条条银带，夏滚道道绿波，秋叠座座金塔，冬砌块块白玉”，形象地描绘出梯田多彩的四季。

LONGSHENG TERRACED FILEDS This scenic spot in Heping Township of Longsheng County is made up by Longji Terraced Fields and Jinkeng Terraced Fields. Like silks and satins, the fields pile up from the foot to the top of the mountains. “Spring sees silvery ribbons floating, Summer finds green ripples rolling, Autumn has bundles of golden crops piled, And heaps of snow look like jades in winter.” These lines give a true portrayal of the four colorful seasons of the terraced fields.

龍勝梯田 棚田風景は龍勝県和平郷内にあり、龍背棚田と金坑棚田の二つに分かれています。棚田の風景は白絹の帯が、麓から山頂にまわりつくように、起伏を重ねながら一気に作り上げたように見えます。「春飄条条銀帯、夏滾道道緑波、秋畳座座金塔、冬砌塊塊白色」という詩は、棚田の豊かな四季の光景を描写しています。

龙脊梯田
Longsheng Terraced Fields
龍脊の棚田

金色家园
A Bumper Harvest
黄金の家園

桂北山寨风情
A Glimpse of a Mountain Village in North Guangxi
桂北の山村

桂北地区生活着壮、苗、瑶、侗等少数民族，这里不仅有如诗如画的山水风光，田园秀色，更有着浓郁纯朴的村寨风情和奇异的民俗。

There live many ethnic minorities in Northern Guangxi, including Zhuang, Miao, Yao, and Dong, etc. Attracting tourists are not only the picturesque landscape there, but simple and honest people with their local customs and traditions.

桂北地区には壮族、苗族、瑶(ヤオ)族、侗(トン)族などの少数民族が住んでいます。この地区には詩や絵になる山水や田園の風景があるばかりでなく、純朴な村落の風情と珍しい民俗習慣が色濃く残っています。

火红的日子
A Busy but Happy Life
真つ赤及暮山し

恭城孔庙
Gongcheng Confucian Temple
恭城の孔廟

全州天湖风光
Quanzhou Heaven Lake
全州天湖

海洋秋色
Autumn Scene of Haiyang
海洋の秋模様

位于桂林市东面的兴安县海洋乡，被称为银杏之乡。每年的12月中旬，当秋霜染过，这里的银杏林便成了金色的海洋，犹如奏响了一段金色的乐章，令人回味无穷。

Located to the east of Guilin city, Haiyang Township in Xing'an County is known to be "a land of Ginkgo". In mid-December each year when autumn frost paints the Ginkgo trees golden, Haiyang turns herself into a wonderland.

興安県海洋郷は桂林市の東南にあり別名「銀杏の里」とも呼ばれています。毎年12月中旬、秋の霜に染まるころ、この辺りの銀杏林は黄金の海に変わります。あたかも金色の楽章を奏でているようです。限りなく回想の世界に引き込まれます。

岩洞 CAVES 洞窟

桂林几乎无山不洞，无洞不奇，据考察，现已发现的岩洞2000多个，其中最为著名的芦笛岩、七星岩、冠岩，以及阳朔县兴坪镇的莲花岩，荔浦县的银子岩、丰鱼岩和灌阳县的黑岩等，近年发现并正在开发的位于永福县的麒麟岩更是充满着神秘的色彩。桂林山水四绝中的“洞奇、石美”二绝可以说是尽在洞中。

In Guilin there is hardly any hill without caves, and all the caves are fantastic. Statistics show that more than 2000 caves have been discovered, among which the most famous are the Reed Flute Cave, the Seven- Star Cave, the Crown Cave, the Lotus Cave, the Silver Cave, the Fengyu Cave and the Dark Cave. The Kylin Cave recently discovered in Yongfu County is especially fantastic, where tourists can find the most characteristic features of the caves and stones in Guilin.

桂林は「山なくして洞なく、洞なくして奇景なし」と言っても過言ではなく、調査によれば、現在2000余りの洞窟が発見されています。その内最も有名なのが、芦笛岩、七星岩、冠岩、及び陽朔県興坪鎮の蓮花岩、荔浦県の銀子岩、豊魚岩、灌陽県の黒岩などです。近年発見され現在開発中のものに、永福県の麒麟岩がありますが、これはさらに神秘的な色彩に満ちています。桂林山水の4つの特色のうち「洞奇、石美」の二つが洞内に揃っています。

莲花岩 · 莲盆浮水
Lotus Cave · Lotus Throne on Water
蓮花岩 · 水江浮かぶ蓮

芦笛岩 · 红罗宝帐
Reed Flute Cave · Red Silks and Satins
芦笛岩 · 赤い薄絹のとばり

丰鱼
Feng
豊魚

芦笛岩 位于桂林市西北部距市区约 7 公里的光明山中，因洞口过去长满可制成笛子的芦荻草而得名。芦笛岩以玲珑剔透，瑰丽神奇著称，洞中的石乳、石笋、石柱、石幔、石花、石瀑等琳琅满目，变化多姿，极尽大自然造化之功，有“大自然艺术之宫”的美誉。

REED FLUTE CAVE Located in Guangming Hill 7 kilometers away from downtown Guilin in the northwest, this cave is reputed as “Nature’s realm of arts”. Well-known for its crystalline stalactites and stalagmites, the cave has a great variety of stone pillars, stone curtains, stone flowers, and stream-like Stalagmites. There used to grow a lot of reeds at the entrance of the cave, from which flutes could be made, and hence the name of Reed Flute Cave.

芦笛岩 桂林西北、市内から 7km 離れた光明山中にあります。昔、洞入口に笛の形をした芦荻草が群生していたことからこの名前がつけられました。芦笛岩はその精巧さと美しさ、不思議さで名高く、洞内は鍾乳洞、石筍、石柱、石幔、石花、石瀑など多種多様で、変化に富み、大自然の造形の妙を尽くしています、そこで「大自然の芸術宮殿」との賞賛を得ています。

芦笛岩 · 龙宫水府
Reed Flute Cave · The Dragon Palace
芦笛岩 · 龍宮水府

麒麟岩 · 凝固的水流
Kylin Cave · Stream-like Stalagmites
麒麟岩 · 凝固した水流

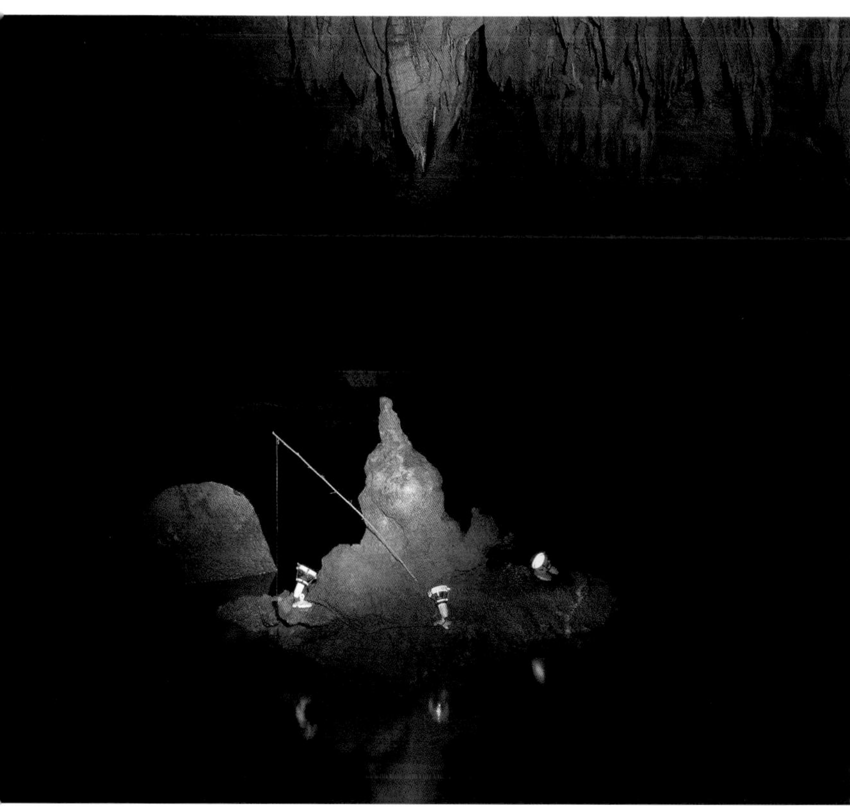

丰鱼岩 · 姜太公钓鱼
Fengyu Cave · An Old Fisherman
豊魚岩 · 姜太公の魚釣り

黑岩 · 群龙迎宾
Dark Cave · Dragons to Welcome the Tourists
黒岩 · 群龍の迎賓

桂林山水的独特之美，不仅吸引了无数的文人墨客和中外摄影家，更是画家们抒写视觉美感、构造精神家园的绝佳胜地，自然的山川之美，古朴的渔村民舍，江岸翠竹扶摇，牧牛散布于绿茵草地，江中筏舟点点、红帆映江，每当日出日落，渔歌唱晚或烟雨朦胧、云绕青峰，光影中的山水情景更是充满诗情画意，画中之景在这似与不似之间，在真实与梦幻之中得到了升华。

Guilin landscape has attracted not only a great number of literary figures and photographers, but also a great many painters. They use their brushes to depict her beauty–pretty hills and clear waters, simple houses in the fishing villages, green bamboo lining up alongside Lijiang River, cowboys herding cattle on the grassland, rafts and red sails drifting on the river, misty waterway and foggy peaks, sunrise and sunset... Realistic or impressionistic, everything in the paintings symbolizes the perfect unity of man and nature.

桂林山水の独自の美しさは、多くの文人墨客や国内外の写真家を魅了しただけでなく、画家たちも美感あふれ、心の楽園をなっているこの景勝地を描写してきました。自然山河の美しさ、古朴な漁民の居宅、川岸の翠竹のざわめき、緑の草地に散らばった牧牛、川に点々とする筏舟、紅帆の水影、日出と日没、漁歌の歌声、青峰を取り巻く雲、光と影の中の情景は詩情画意に満ちており、画中の風景は真実と夢幻の中で昇華されています。

象山春早
Early Spring of Elephant Hill
象山の春

漓江清晓
Morning Scene of Lijiang River
漓江朝の調べ

漓江烟云图
Lijiang River in Mist
漓江にかかる雲

漓江百里图卷(局部)
Scroll of the Picture Gallery of Lijiang River
漓江百里図(局部)

雪迷溪山
Snow Scene
南渓山の雪

雾雨清漓
Lijiang River in Misty Drizzle
深い川霧

夏江雾雨
Lijiang River in Summer Mist
夏の川霧

魂系漓江烟水路
Breathtaking Lijiang River
漓江の川霧

漓江之晨
Dawn of Lijiang River
漓江の朝

烟雨漓江
Lijiang River in Misty Rain
雨の漓江

春溪山水图
Spring Stream
春の渓山

漓江清韵
Tranquil Lijiang River
漓江の風景

清漓牧歌
Herding by Lijiang River
江畔牧牛

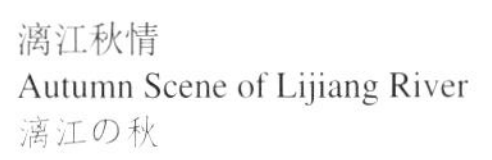

漓江秋情
Autumn Scene of Lijiang River
漓江の秋

春江水
Lijiang River in Spring
春の川

图书在版编目(CIP)数据
桂林胜境／漓江出版社编 .—桂林：漓江出版社，2004.1
ISBN 7 - 5407 - 3259 - 8

Ⅰ.桂... Ⅱ.漓... Ⅲ.桂林—概况—画册 Ⅳ. K926.73-64

中国版本图书馆CIP数据核字（2004）第001638号

桂林胜境 GUILIN SHENGJING

编　　者／土　原
书名题字／阳太阳
撰　　文／邓淇文 李伟光
封面、封底摄影／文绍军、谭邵江
内封摄影／黄富旺
内文摄影／李会先 谭邵江 韦毅刚等
策划责编／李伟光
装帧设计／土　原
英文翻译／陆巧玲
日文翻译／稲岡安則
出版发行／漓江出版社
社　　址／广西桂林市南环路22号
邮政编码：541002
电话：(0773)2863971　2863978
传真：(0773)2802018
E-mail: ljcbs@public.glptt.gx.cn
印　　刷／深圳雅昌彩色印刷有限公司
开　　本／787×1092　1/16
印　　张／6.25
版　　次／2004年10月第1版第1次印刷
印　　数／8000
ISBN 7-5407-3259-8/J·171
(00530)

如有印装质量问题　请与出版社营销部调换